JOEL C. GRAHAM

CHESS
FOR BEGINNERS

Discover Essential Tactics, Learn Expert
Strategies, and Play Like a Pro

The Ultimate Guide to Mastering the Game From Scratch

CHESS FOR BEGINNERS

The Ultimate Guide to Mastering the Game From Scratch | Discover Essential Tactics, Learn Expert Strategies, and Play Like a Pro

First Edition August 2023

© Copyright 2023 by Joel C. Graham - All rights reserved.

This document is geared towards providing exact and reliable information regarding the topic and issue covered. The publication is sold with the idea that the publisher is not required to render accounting, officially permitted, or otherwise qualified services. If advice is necessary, legal, or professional, a practiced individual in the profession should be ordered.

- From a Declaration of Principles, which was accepted and approved equally by a Committee of the American Bar Association and a Committee of Publishers and Associations.

In no way is it legal to reproduce, duplicate, or transmit any part of this document in either electronic means or in printed format. Recording of this publication is strictly prohibited, and any storage of this document is not allowed unless with written permission from the publisher. All rights reserved.

The information provided herein is stated to be truthful and consistent in that any liability, in terms of inattention or otherwise, by any usage or abuse of any policies, processes, or directions contained within is the solitary and utter responsibility of the recipient reader. Under no circumstances will any legal responsibility or blame be held against the publisher for any reparation, damages, or monetary loss due to the information herein, either directly or indirectly.

Respective authors own all copyrights not held by the publisher.

The information herein is offered for informational purposes solely and is universal as so. The presentation of the information is without a contract or any type of guarantee assurance.

The trademarks that are used are without any consent, and the publication of the trademark is without permission or backing by the trademark owner. All trademarks and brands within this book are for clarifying purposes only and are owned by the owners themselves, not affiliated with this document.

This document is geared towards providing exact and reliable information regarding the topic and issue covered. The publication is sold with the idea that the publisher is not required to render accounting, officially permitted, or otherwise, qualified services. If advice is necessary, legal, or professional, a practiced individual in the profession should be ordered. - From a Declaration of Principles, which was accepted and approved equally by a Committee of the American Bar Association and a Committee of Publishers and Associations. In no way is it legal to reproduce, duplicate, or transmit any part of this document in either electronic means or in printed format. Recording of this publication is strictly prohibited, and any storage of this document is not allowed unless with written permission from the publisher. All rights reserved. The information provided herein is stated to be truthful and consistent, in that any liability, in terms of inattention or otherwise, by any usage or abuse of any policies, processes, or directions contained within is the solitary and utter responsibility of the recipient reader. Under no circumstances will any legal responsibility or blame be held against the publisher for any reparation, damages, or monetary loss due to the information herein, either directly or indirectly. Respective authors own all copyrights not held by the publisher. The information herein is offered for informational purposes solely and is universal as so. The presentation of the information is without a contract or any type of guarantee assurance. The trademarks that are used are without any consent, and the publication of the trademark is without permission or backing by the trademark owner. All trademarks and brands within this book are for clarifying purposes only and are owned by the owners themselves, not affiliated with this document.

CHESS FOR BEGINNERS

The Ultimate Guide to Mastering the Game
From Scratch | Discover Essential Tactics,
Learn Expert Strategies, and Play Like a Pro

JOEL C. GRAHAM

TABLE OF CONTENTS

INTRODUCTION 7

CHAPTER 1
INTRODUCTION TO CHESS... 11

1.1 History of Chess...12
1.2 The Original Champions of the World 15
1.3 Benefits of Chess...20
1.4 How to Approach Learning Chess....................................23

CHAPTER 2
HOW TO SETUP A CHESS BOARD........................... 27

2.1 The Goal of the Game 28
2.2 Description of the Chessmen...31
2.3 Setting Up the Board...39

CHAPTER 3
CHESS NOTATION AND TERMINOLOGY 43

3.1 Algebraic Notation...44
3.2 Chess Terminology 45

CHAPTER 4
ESSENTIAL RULES AND GAMEPLAY 51

4.1 Rules of the Game...52
4.2 Standard Chess Regulations and Procedures 57
4.3 Etiquette and Sportsmanship in Chess..........................59

CHAPTER 5
BASIC OPENING PRINCIPLES.................................. 63

5.1 King's Pawn Openings 66

5.2 Queen's Pawn Opening 69

5.3 Flanking Holes 71

5.4 Choosing Your Opening..73

CHAPTER 6
BASIC TACTICS... 75

6.1 How to Choose the Right Openings...............................76

6.2 Double Attack..78

6.3 Discovered Attacks 79

6.4 Skewers and Hooks...81

CHAPTER 7
STRATEGIC PLANNING AND POSITIONAL
UNDERSTANDING... 83

7.1 Position Evaluation 84

CHAPTER 8
ENDGAME TACTICS... 91

8.1 Endgame Tactics and Moves...94

CHAPTER 9
CHESS MINDSET: DEVELOPING THE
RIGHT MENTAL ATTITUDE 99

CHAPTER 10
READING THE OPPONENT:
UNDERSTANDING STRATEGIES AND
PATTERNS 105

CONCLUSION 117

INTRODUCTION

Chess is a game where you can win even after making a mistake. You may still prevail even if you commit an error. In most games, both sides make several errors, and the loser is the one who makes the last significant blunder that results in a checkmate. And the legendary world champions are successful in producing some terrible motions.

Beginners often make mistakes, frequently losing pieces inadvertently, but with a little assistance from the opposition, they can always survive or even win. However, even a little error can fail in stronger opposition. Your main objective is to minimize or completely avoid mistakes.

A move in chess can be broken down into three distinct parts. Introductory period actions are planned to gain an advantage against the opponent. The second stage is when players compete for position on the board and control via attacks, retorts, and defenses. The endgame, the last phase, is where the kings are used. Saving the king becomes the goal, and checking the opponent becomes the plan.

Both players will collect pieces as the game progresses. Each participant should attempt to capture more pieces than their opponent to win the game. Overanalyzing might put the component at risk of being accidentally captured. Such a seductive capture is called "En Prise" or "In Taking." However, on occasion, players willfully arrange their pieces in their opponent's direction as a part of a plan to trap them when they capture a piece.

So, why play chess? Chess is a game that is both fun and mentally taxing. Chess is a game that will give you enjoyment if you like logic puzzles, riddles, puzzles that require problem-solving, and other similar activities. If none of these above appeals to you, chess may still be enjoyable.

Additionally, although chess is linked to analytical thinking, it has an aesthetic component. Many Grandmasters have received praise throughout the history of this beautiful game for their unusually interesting chess strategies that include surprising pairings and masterful piece sacrifices. But we shall discuss these in greater detail later on in the book.

Is chess challenging? Very! Is learning it a challenge? Many players gloss over the difficulties involved. It will take you only a short time to understand the game's fundamental principles since they are fairly straightforward. The challenging part of learning chess is becoming a competent player. It may take time to become proficient at playing chess due to the unlimited number of movements one can make at each round. This book will teach you about these things, including chess tactics, strategies, dos and don'ts, pattern detection, opening and endgame theory, and comprehension of unique playing patterns.

But, in the end, playing the game is the only effective method to learn it. Your ability to play the game becomes better the more you play. The only way to improve as a chess player is to make mistakes repeatedly and learn from each one. Losing games and learning from them is the greatest way to improve as a chess player.

Chapter 1

INTRODUCTION TO CHESS

In chess, success usually comes through failing. If you avoid making mistakes, you cannot lose. In most games, both sides make numerous mistakes, and the loser is the one who makes the final, decisive blunder that results in a checkmate.

Both chess players make silly mistakes. The great World Champions have also been successful in producing some truly horrible gestures.

Despite making numerous blunders and accidentally losing pieces, beginners can always pull through and even win with minimal help from their opponents.

But when up against sturdier opposition, failure might result from the smallest of slip-ups. To better oneself as a player. Avoiding or minimizing your flaws should be your top priority.

1.1 History of Chess

The history of chess is rich and illustrious. Timekeeping devices were nonexistent, and uniform coinage did not appear until the nineteenth century.

After the first major tournaments were played and different playing styles had matured, the official world championship ·title was established in the late 19th century. The first book on openings was published in 1843, but the modern idea didn't develop until the early to mid-20th century. It wasn't until the latter end of the twentieth century that computerized search engines and databases became commonplace.

Where Did the Game of Chess Develop?

The Indian game chaturanga predates the sixth century A.D. and is widely credited as the ancestor of modern chess. Over the succeeding years, the game expanded throughout Asia and Europe, developing into the chess we know today sometime in the 16th century. He didn't create the movie that bears his name, but he did publish an analysis of it in a book in 1561. Lopez, a pioneer of early 20th-century chess theory, recommended playing with the sun in your opponent's eyes.

Theories of the Game and Its Evolution During the 19th century

This book not only included several novel approaches to beginning the game (like as the defense that bears his name) but also Philidor's famed defense in rook and pawn endgames, which is still in use today. Philidor's now-iconic "The pawns are the soul of chess" remark had its debut in this publication.

As chess's global popularity grew, so did the number of rules and pieces include in each set. Chess sets were far from standard before the 1850s. In 1849 a London-based producer of games and toys debuted Nathaniel Cooke's fresh take on the chess set. Howard Staunton, the greatest player of his era, recommended these exact pieces. The Staunton pattern, a contemporary design for chess pieces, was immediately adopted by players and clubs around the world. Even today, tournament chess sets are expected to use the Staunton pieces or a variant thereof.

Chess clocks were first used in tournaments in the 19th century. A single game might take up to 14 hours before the widespread use of chess clocks. The modernization of chess encounters and championships required the establishment of the proper facilities, which was offered by the establishment of standards of the chess pieces and the introduction of chess monitors.

The game of chess itself advanced tremendously in the nineteenth century. The most well-known games from this era were swashbuckling attacks, as effective defensive strategies were not yet known. If one player wasn't violently sacrificing pieces to checkmate the other, the game would be boring. The American chess player Paul Morphy emerged during this time of aggressive play.

Morphy was the personification of these idealistic and combative attacks on reality. Morphy won every match he played in Europe, including those against the world's top players, with the exception of Howard Staunton. Morphy blew away a number of experts, including Anderssen, Paulsen, Harrwitz, and a few others. Morphy uses a "everything but the kitchen sink" approach to defeat his foes. A timeless masterpiece of a game.

1.2 The Original Champions of the World

Morphy had already departed from the game by the time Wilhelm Steinitz became famous, therefore the two never met. The influence of Steinitz's game theory, notably his dislike of aggression, is recognized even now. In order to win more slowly, he chose to take the widely-offered gambit piece and subsequently to close the position. Steinitz was the first declared world champion in 1886 since no one else could match him in positional play.

In 1894, Emanuel Lasker soundly defeated Steinitz (10-5), ending Steinitz's reign as world champion. Three years later, in a rematch, Lasker won again, this time by a score of 10-2. Lasker's reign as chess world champion would be the longest at 27 years.

Following the examples set by Steinitz and Lasker, positional chess gained significant traction. Up until the early 20th century, the standard opening strategy was to push your pawns toward the center of the board. The Ruy Lopez, Giuoco Piano, Queen's Gambit, French Defense, and Four Knights' Game were the most frequently played openings. The two sides progressively try to gain advantages in space, important squares, diagonals, and files from these quiet openings.

In 1921, Jose Raul Capablanca became the third world champion after defeating Lasker. The way that Capablanca had played the game continues to be viewed to be the best way to understand structural play. He avoided tactical tangles whenever possible, preferring instead to capture a seemingly slight edge and then exploit it to victory in the endgame. His expertise in the late stages of a game was unparalleled. Capablanca's endgame method is so sound that even the strongest chess computers can discover very few mistakes in it. Capablanca is widely regarded as a chess great despite the short duration of his reign as world champion (six years).

Hypermodernism, a new school of thinking, penetrated elite chess in the 1920s. The goal is to use minor pieces to exert influence on the center rather than merely occupying it with pawns. The games and theories of the next generation of chess greats—including Nimzovich, Efim, Reti, and Grunfeld—highlighted these novel concepts. During this time, numerous well-known openings, such as the Indian Defenses, the Grunfeld, and the Benoni, saw the formation of new openings and development schemes.

The Alekhine's Defense (after the fourth world champion, Alexander Alekhine) is one of the most innovative moves in chess. The idea of this defense is to tempt White into advancing his core pawns, which will then leave him vulnerable to an attack from the black side. Alekhine is now mostly regarded as the first player to employ a dynamic playing style, one in which he could alternate between playing extremely skillfully and aggressively and playing quietly and positionally. From 1927 until his defeat by Max Euwe in 1935, he was recognized as the best boxer in the world. The rematch was won by Alekhine in 1937, and he retained his title until his untimely passing in 1946. He was the only person to ever hold the title of chess world champion and later passed away.

The Soviet Union's Impenetrable 20th Century Hold

With only two exceptions, every world champion from 1927 through 2006 was a player from the Soviet Union or Russia. The dominance of the title was demonstrated by the chess greats of the 20th and early 21st centuries, including Alekhine, Mikhail, Vassily, Mikhail, Tigran, Spassky, Anatoly and Garry Kasparov, and Vladimir Kramnik. The aforementioned chess greats' playing styles are polar opposites of one another. Every style is represented, from the positional mastery of Karpov, Petrosian, Smyslov, and Kramnik to the extreme ferocity of Tal's attacks and the dynamic prowess of Alekhine, Botvinnik, and Kasparov.

Following Alekhine's reign as world champion, Mikhail Botvinnik won the title in 1948. Not only was this the first time the world championship wasn't decided by a single match (a quintuple match system was used due to the absence of a reigning world champion), but it also marked the first time that FIDE would oversee the event (something they still do today). From 1948 through 1963 (with two one-year breaks), Botvinnik was the world champion.

Botvinnik's dynamic talents and iron logic made him a formidable opponent. He could adapt his play to his opponent like a chameleon. Although Botvinnik lost the 1957 championship match to Vassily Smyslov, the regulations of the time allowed for a rematch the following year. Botvinnik defeated Smyslov in a rematch for the championship in 1958. Botvinnik was defeated by Mikhail Tal for the championship in

1960. Botvinnik defeated Tal in a rematch in 1961, nevertheless. When Botvinnik lost a match to Tigran Petrosian in 1963, FIDE amended the rules such that he could no longer demand a rematch the following year.

Botvinnik, after his lengthy term as world champion, became one of the most prestigious chess instructors of all time. He is the only one who can say they trained Karpov, Kasparov, and Kramnik, all future world champions. He also contributed to computer science and is remembered as a pioneer in the field of computer chess.

After beating Botvinnik in 1963, Tigran Petrosian became the ninth player to hold that title. He used a positional approach and was known for his brilliant trade sacrifices. In 1966, Petrosian successfully defended his championship against Boris Spassky. Spassky faced Petrosian for the second time for the world championship in 1969, three years after he had won the candidates cycle again. Spassky won the 1969 match against Petrosian, making him the tenth and current world champion. After three years, Spassky would lose the title to Bobby Fischer in a historic match.

Between 1970 and 1972, it appeared like nobody on the planet could stop him. He won a first-to-six Candidates' Match against Mark Taimanov in 1971. Fischer started out the match by winning all six of their games. A few months later, he did it all over again, this time winning six matches in a row against Bent Larsen. Both of these are two activities that haven't ever been accomplished in the past.

Even those who knew nothing about chess were enthralled by the 1972 showdown between Fischer and Spassky. This wasn't only the most important world championship game in history; it also had major geopolitical implications. In addition to their Cold War conflict, the United States and the Soviet Union were also engaged in a battle for chess dominance. Fischer was a nightmare to work with, as seen by his first game loss, a drawn endgame ruined by a bizarre elementary error. Then, after noticing issues in the arena during the second game, he bowed out. Spassky jumped off to an early 2-0 lead, putting Fischer in a deep hole from the outset. Fischer staged one of the greatest comebacks in chess history, prevailing 12.5 games to 8.5 in a best-of-24 match. That match's sixth round is considered to be to be among the best-known contests that has ever been completed.

In 2005, it became widely accepted that computers are far more capable than humans. This was because the supercomputer Hydra handily beat Michael Adams, who was rated number seven in the world at the time. With 5.5 points from a possible 6, Hydra was victorious in the match. The power of computer engines kept improving. The estimated ELO of Stockfish, a popular open-source engine, is around 3400. AlphaZero, a new chess program, dispatched Stockfish in a 100-game match 2017. A thousand-game battle with time odds was the latest arena in which AlphaZero triumphed over Stockfish in early 2018.

When using computers for analysis, research, and opening theory, humans also become more powerful. Since his 2013 victory over Viswanathan Anand, Carlsen has held the title of world champion and has been considered the best player in the world. He started off the year by competing in and winning each of the four of the competitions in which he participated. His current classical rating is 2876, and his all-time high was 2882 (attained in 2014). He is widely considered to be the most skilled athlete in the history of the sport.

1.3 Benefits of Chess

The game of chess is popular around the globe. Playing each other in a cerebral war of wits, this age-old game unites individuals from all areas of life. Decisions must be made on the go while also considering future options. The game fascinates all players since their decisions constantly shift in response to their opponent's moves.

However, chess has many more benefits than just entertainment. You might only be aware of a number of the benefits of participating in this time-honored pastime. Remember these advantages the next time you sit down for a friendly match with a friend, a lesson, or a competitive encounter. They could inspire you to make playing a regular part of your life.

Creative Problem-Solving Skills Can Be Honed by Playing Chess

You may not become an artist by playing chess, but you will get more imaginative. Because you must actively think about how to attack your opponent and organize your movements, it challenges your thinking in novel ways. Learning to take calculated risks and think creatively on the chessboard can help you in all aspects of your life.

Playing the Game Increases Confidence

Chess players gain confidence in themselves outside of the game as their knowledge and abilities improve. A player's first victory over a formidable foe reinforces the idea that persistent effort pays off.

That assurance can be taken into regular life. It's a terrific way to develop confidence in both young and old.

People who play chess often report having greater fun with other creative pursuits, because the game challenges both the right and left sides of the brain.

The Game of Chess Is a Great Teacher of Patience

Learning to be patient is challenging in today's fast-paced society. Players are compelled to develop patience in chess because they must wait for their opponents to make their moves. Only a few other games provide growth opportunities and encourage players to take it slow and deliberate.

Players are given ample time to consider their options, resulting in a leisurely pace. Players must consider their immediate next action and their potential subsequent moves. Spend time to play with the competition of chessboard if you do not wish to see rapid progression of your defeat.

Chess Teaches Sportsmanship

Learning sportsmanship is another advantage of playing chess. irrespective of how close the probabilities might seem, always is going to be a winner as well as a loser at the end of the day. No of the outcome, players must learn to behave graciously.

Players who view each game as a learning experience are less likely to throw tantrums and feel irritated when they lose at chess. When athletes develop good sportsmanship, they benefit not only on the field but also in the classroom and on the job.

Chess Enhances Memory and Recall

One of chess' many positive health effects is enhanced recall and memory. Competitors ought to give some thought to their decisions. Players are also required to predict the maneuvers of their adversary. School-aged children that play can benefit from the game's emphasis on memorization and recall, an ability that will serve them well throughout their lives.

1.4 How to Approach Learning Chess

These methods of memory can also be used to boost performance in the game of chess. They can mentally play back games and replicate the results on their boards.

Chess training takes a lot of time. You must learn key positions and sequences, including checkmate patterns and endgame approaches, study strategy concepts and develop your tactical talents. But where is this of greater significance than in the beginning?

That is to say, multiple grandmasters and other talented players have spent endless hours determining the best opening moves to play, and we would be very prudent to at least take note of what they've discovered. Furthermore, memorization might save you time and difficulty in a genuine game. Try to think of a different concept instead of the Sicily idea that is now accepted!

Find the Right Positions

Before we get to the major advice, there is one crucial caveat. As previously stated, investigating vacancies takes time, so save your valuable time on the right one! It is such an essential topic that it will be the subject of its blog entry.

For one thing, you would not offer hypermodern openings to a beginning or lower-intermediate player. This includes any opening that begins with 1.Nf3. This is because these openings are intricate and demand extreme precision, and they frequently can transpose to other openings.

It's also critical to find and stick with a good beginning. It is only advisable to continuously change openings once you reach a higher level. As a result, you should look for and perfect an introduction that interests you. While being well-rounded has certain advantages, consistency is far more crucial in this scenario, at least at the starting and intermediate levels.

Understand the Pawn Structures Related to an Opening

As previously stated, memory is vital, but understanding the logic behind the movements and overall plan is much more critical. It is impossible to recall every potential variation written. In any case, no introductory course or book will prepare you for every variation, so you'll need some sort of master strategy to serve as a guiding light when you're unsure what to do.

Studying and playing games requires repetition.

This may appear to be two separate points, yet it is a symbiotic relationship! You should go over your openings several times while studying and playing.

Chessable is the ideal tool for studying openings, which is why it was partly invented. You can use spaced repetition to test your grasp of the maneuvers and learn their theory.

However, putting your knowledge into practice is equally critical, as practice will depart from theory at some point.

But don't just go on a blitz frenzy when you play. Following all of the matches, set aside some time to think about the manner in which the tournament started out. Is this what your Chessable instructor or coach advised? Did you mess up the sequence? Is that even something covered in the course? Take time to get things done properly so you don't develop undesirable habits. It pays significant long-term dividends.

You have the option of writing a comment in the framework if there is nothing which you cannot comprehend or if you stumble upon an alternative which is not covered in the material. The teacher will typically respond fairly soon to deal with the concern if they see it. In many situations, your question will be used to improve the course in a future update, which will also benefit others.

You can also ask questions on the Chessable discussion forums, where you will certainly receive prompt and polite assistance from a very enthusiastic group.

Examine Descriptive Annotated Master Games

The final advice is to play through some master games with that opening. Examine how the pros approach that opening and their plan. It is also beneficial to memorize some - by doing so, you can construct a mental library of positions and methods that you can use when playing across the board.

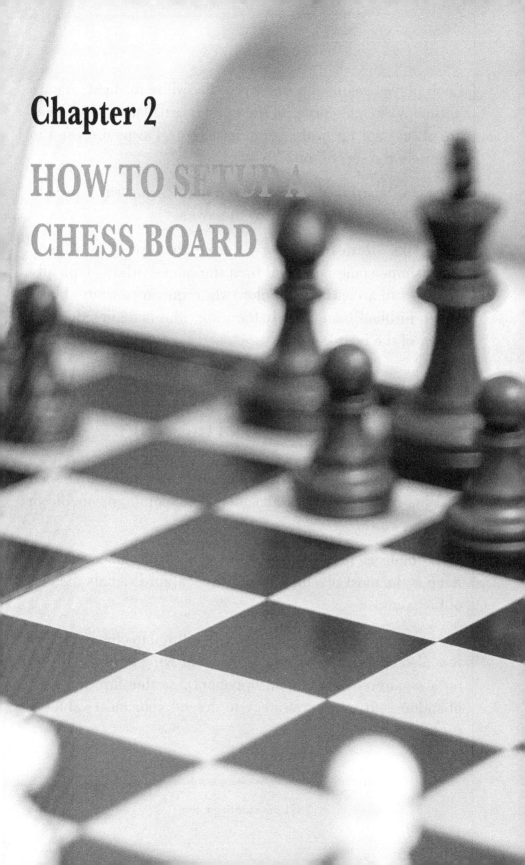

Chapter 2

HOW TO SET UP A
CHESS BOARD

Each player begins the game with the white (or light) square in the lower right corner of the chessboard. The chess pieces are always set up in the same formation. Pawns are used to complete the second rank (row).

The chessboard is always prepared in the same way. The second rank (row) is completed with pawns.

The rooks are in the corners, the knights are next to them, the bishops come next, and then the queen, who is typically depicted in a contrasting color (white queen in white, black queen in black), and finally the king, who is depicted in the center of the board.

2.1 The Goal of the Game

The object of chess is to corner your opponent's King such that his or her King is under attack, immobile, or unable to help the Pawn.

Checkmate is the term for this result. Remember that the King is the most pivotal piece, as his capture signals the end of the game.

Remember that the King cannot be captured in chess and that it is also against the rules to place your King in check (move on a square covered by an opponent), as this forces you to abandon your current strategy to defend your most valuable piece.

How to Check: A to Z

Put a piece in the path of an adversary to prevent them from reaching the King.

Capture: Take control of the piece assaulting the King.

Chess is unusual among board games because it can be played without necessarily having a victor and a loser. Players can formally concede a game by setting down their King or exclaiming, "I resign!" In chess, there are six distinct kinds of draws:

Agreement

After making your move, you may propose a draw to your opponent. When the other player accepts, the game is over. When an opponent declines a surrender, play continues.

Not Enough Information:

The game ends when neither side has enough pieces to checkmate the other's King.

"The 50-Move Rule"

After fifty movements have been completed with neither an opponent's pawn being relocated or an opponent's piece being taken over, either player can state that the outcome is a match. This scenario could be proven only with the moves recorded or with an impartial observer present.

Stalemate:

The game is over when neither player's King is in check, and no valid movements remain.

Always Verifying:

The game is over when one player checks the King three times and copies the same location each time.

It's a tie if you copy the same location three times in a row without making any changes.

Said, Board

The checkerboard is 8 by 8, giving 64 playing areas. Produced by contrasting 32-square panels of light and dark. Set the board in front of you; whether you're playing White or Black, the bottom right corner must always be illuminated. The letters and numbers that go around the perimeter of a chessboard give each square a name. To participate in a chess conversation, it is necessary to jot down your moves, and the names given to the courts serve the same purpose as coordinates in a coordinate system.

For clarity, let's define "chess conversation" as discussing a position with another person, such as a friend or chess teacher, and giving that position a name. For instance, the Pawn on d5 may have been captured by my Knight on c3.

In a chess conversation, you should also use these terms:

Files

The board's eight horizontal columns are separated by vertical lines called files. The letters A through H represent the alphabetical order of the files.

Ranks

The ranks are the lines across the board separating the bottom and top rows.

Queen's and Kings' Reverses

We can also divide the board in half vertically: QUEENSIDE and KINGSIDE. Queenside includes the a, b, c, and d files. Kingside consists of the e, f, g, and h files. We might use one of these terms in a sentence, such as, "I castled my King on the queenside."

2.2 Description of the Chessmen

Pawn

Named after the legendary Pawnee tribe of North America's Great Plains. The Cheyenne accurately named this kind of warrior "The Huntsmen of the Plains," and the Sioux acknowledged them.

With its unique ability to travel diagonally across the board and capture other pieces, the pawn stands out among the other board components. The instrument may seem weak, but it may become one of your most powerful pieces with strategic planning. Except for their initial move, in which they can move two squares, pawns can only move in one direction at a time. The instrument may only move diagonally to capture another piece, never forward, backward, or to the side. If there's an intervening piece between the pawn and the target, the pawn can't go to it or take it.

Over time, the Greyhounds dwindled in numbers until they were the Pawnee tribe least represented in war groups. While dispersing across the Great Plains, many scattered bands of Indians and traders fell victim to violent attacks. The Greyhounds were ordered to attack the Latrine of the Kiowa, their archrivals, and abuse it like a nest of prairie fowl would be treated by a pack of foxes.

Gagged men were still among the living. Wounded men were ruthlessly executed. Greyhounds captured civilians, including women and children. They would take the fur and hides from the captive's animals and devour the meat.

Before 1879, only legends were spoken about the incredible power and prowess of the Greyhounds.

Rooks

Originating with the chess piece Rook. Enemies often fail to notice rooks because they believe a rook's presence is enough to win a battle.

But the Sioux could notice even the smallest changes and anticipate when an attack would begin. The Sioux were known for being careless around their villages and unwary of troop movements, so their foes often took these assumptions as gospel. Even when the Sioux were poised to launch an attack, their opponents typically saw through their ploy. The Sioux sang and called to their horses, hawks, and dogs before they left camp. They'd also be watching the local flora and fauna, which may give away the presence of American troops long before they were seen.

Knights

Originating with the chess piece known as "Knights." The chess knight is one of the most mobile pieces and can compete effectively with any other element. The best part about knights is that they can roam the board and hop from piece to piece. Likewise, the Sioux were capable of similar feats. In one case, the Sioux ran upon a telegraph crew and utilized the opportunity to send bogus messages back to the telegraph headquarters. For several days, they avoided detection.

Bishops

Originating with the chess piece known as "Bishops." Bishops rely on knights to stand by. The caps on these items are reminiscent of the hats a bishop might wear (how fitting!). Bishops move like rooks since they can switch squares but do so in a diagonal pattern rather than following the straight line of the rows and columns. Bishops are free to change roles as much as they choose but are restricted to playing just one diagonal role at a time.

Bishops are restricted since they can only rest in a square of the same color as the one from which they first moved. Their breadth, however, has been verified to be an advantage.

The constraints for mobility who are placed on the knight of the game are among the most peculiar of all the pieces used in chess. They can only go up or down one space, across one room, or one area and two spaces horizontally, giving the appearance of an "L" as their final movement. Because it allows for a unique and significant design that can only sometimes be avoided, this precise movement pattern provides both advantages and disadvantages for the participant and the opponent. While you're at it, try making some more content.

The bishop is one of the most underappreciated chess pieces. The enemy king is constantly under attack from the bishops. They can also be employed tactically to lure the enemy king into the center of the board, where he or she can be more easily attacked. The bishops will then surprise their opponent and kill their King. King Sioux had a well-known Trickster tradition and could do just that. The term "Ghost Dance" was coined to describe this ritual. The Sioux sometimes disguised themselves as enemy soldiers or used masks to fool their opponents. A Sioux warrior posed as an elderly man and was given shelter by the Union army. He hid behind enemy lines for months, where he sought a Christian among the ranks. The Sioux reacted violently when one soldier admitted yes and exposed himself.

Kings

Originating with the chess piece King. King, the King's largest selection, moves to the bishop on the right side of the board. The king Kingravel in any direction, but only one row at a time, making it a weak piece. However, because kings seize, this makes them the most powerful work on the board in the shortest time.

The Sioux were such a formidable force that they could identify their opponents' King and Kingow discord in his court. They were also quite capable of picking a suitable location and timing for the battle. The Sioux often "fight behind their lines," or lure the adversary into their territory and ambush them there.

Queens

Queen is a chess piece's name, hence the name. The queen's role is among the most difficult to understand in chess. In the match of games of chess queen is the most powerful component in the match. She is able to move in whichever way she chooses, just like a knight does, because she enjoys full autonomy in her mobility. As long as she stays on her designated route, she can go in any order until she reaches her set square. Queens were common among the Sioux. There were grandma, aunts, uncles, cousins, nieces, nephews, and cousins. They were forced to negotiate the terrain of a culture that was predominated by men. The men's brutality was something they had to put up with. They were all compelled to implement the same policies and conquer the same regions. They were tasked with protecting the lodge, caring for the kids, reining in the wild horses, and securing the portable lodging.

2.3 Setting Up the Board

Setting up a functional chessboard without breaking a sweat Chess is both humorous and challenging.

Chessboard horizontal

The most important thing is to get your page set up properly. This may seem random, but the chessboard's function is one of the crucial factors in ensuring the boards are in the right place.

Place the parts.

The knights resemble steeds. Bishops are those pieces that have a "frown" groove on top. A "crown" sits atop the queen, the second-tallest music in the set.

Your current adversary's (dark sides) environment is comparable.

The most notable variation is that while playing with dark pieces from left to right, the king or sovereign always goes first.

You'll perform the necessary analysis and testing in less than a second. Obviously, the smallest piece on the board is the pedestrian, who occupies the second row from the bottom for both sides.

As was mentioned previously, chess is a time-honored game of strategy and tactic. It's a difficult board game played with 64 squares and colors of chance. These squares can be either light or dark. Typically, the parts are black, and the white performs the initial motions at the traditional start. The sixteen parts of each ingredient are as follows:

- There are eight infantrymen.
- Two rooks, or castles.
- Two high priests, or bishops.
- Two guard knights.
- Two royal people (King and Queen)

The chessboard can be arranged in numerous ways, but one common method involves shifting eight squares to one side and right.

Set the following preferences in your gamers:

In the row directly below you:

- Location of a Rook at each end.
- Place a bishop in the center of the board after every set of rooks.
- Now, put a single night within easy reach of each Bishop.
- Find the king in the square off to one side.
- The ultimate rectangle is where you should put your queen.

In the first square, from left to right, place one Rook, one Bishop, one Knight, and eight Pioneers. The infantry's mission is to provide absolute protection for the king.

Putting the lord on the OPPOSITE area of shading will help you remember where the king and queen are hiding. If the king is white, he could be practicing black art. See the kind guy if it's dark outside. Every instance is the same.

During the game, the pieces are passed around in a specific order. Here's a rundown of how each part can be moved:

- The snare may travel through any number of horizontal or vertical squares with equal ease, but it can't evade individual shapes.
- Bishops can move from corner to corner, occupying any number of squares but they must avoid specific areas.
- After passing two squares horizontally or vertically, a knight can pass a court into an "L" formation of any orientation. The knight is the most vital component in the game because of its ability to jump.
- At any time, the king can send a rectangle along any road. The "château" advancement is an important outlier, as it allows the rook to move two squares toward the ruler and the lord to move two squares in the other direction.
- The end outcome is an adversarial position for the Rook and King. As long as neither the euro nor the lord has moved before, it may usually be finished utilizing the two sides of the board.
- Although she is able to walk in any particular direction and through a multitude of neighboring rectangles, the queen is unable to hop.

Throughout the first stage, commuters will be able to move through two or three squares; throughout the subsequent levels, they will be able to move across one rectangle.

Your "military" will square off against the enemy when everything is set up properly. The purpose of the competition is to either take control of the enemy prince or remove him from the board. A pioneer in this field who was among the first to accomplish this goal.

Chapter 3

CHESS NOTATION AND TERMINOLOGY

Keeping score in chess notation makes it easy to review past games, whether to improve your skill or just to show off to your friends. When you make the winning move in your next game, try writing it out in chess notation and see how much more enjoyable it is.

3.1 Algebraic Notation

Algebraic notation is the most frequent and easiest to learn chess notation. It provides alphabetical and numeric labeling of the chess board's grid.

White starts at the far end of the board, at rank 1; black at rank 8. White's left to right, the files (or columns) are labeled.

Additionally, the following parts employ capitalization:

- K: King
- Q: Majesty
- R: Rook
- B: Bishop
- K: Knave
- Pawn (albeit the letter P is often omitted from notation due to tradition)

3.2 Chess Terminology

The Parts

THE ROYAL

The monarchy serves as the primary protagonist. The game's goal is to win by eliminating your opponent's King. In each direction, the King can advance one square. Checkmate for the King might never come. The game begins with one King for each player.

The Queen: This is the strongest piece in the game. As long as she doesn't run into any obstacles, she can go an unlimited number of squares in any direction. The players all start given a queen as their starting point at the beginning of the contest.

THE ROOK

If its path is not blocked, the rook can travel up to eight squares vertically or sixteen squares horizontally.

BISHOP

The head of the bishop is able to travel across a limitless quantity of spaces if the opposite pathway it would normally take is vacant. At the outset, each player is given two bishops, one to place on either side of their King and Queen.

The Knight

The Knight has a unique ability in chess since it can double jump. It travels two squares in either the horizontal or vertical direction before turning right and covering the final square. When the Knight moves from one square to another, it always stops on the square of the opposing hue. Between their bishops and rooks, each player begins the game with two knights.

The Pawn

The Pawn always advances forward and never retreats, although it captures on the diagonal. Except for the initial turn, when it can choose between a one-square and two-square advance, it always travels one square at a time. The game begins with eight pawns per player.

Chess Terminology: The Outcomes

Check

Whenever the monarch is in a situation where he might have been taken captive, the necessary condition is met.

Checkmate

Once the monarch is unable advance any farther, the game is said to be in achieving checkmate.

STALEMATE

A deadlock happens whenever the person who has the chance it is to advance is unable to move legally because he is trapped in a position in which his dominant position is not underneath inspection, and he does not have any other acceptable options accessible to him. In the scenario that there is no clear winner, the game goes on forever. The competition did not end with a winner being determined.

RESIGN

To resign is to admit defeat and give up the game. Turning one's King over is a common symbol of resignation.

Chess Terminology: Special Moves

CASTLE

After moving two squares toward one of its rooks, the King switches sides with the rook. To the castle, the King moves two squares on the first rank toward one of the original rooks, and then that rook moves onto the square the King just vacated. The act of casting is permitted if neither of the available sectors surrounding the ruler as the hitting rook have been taken over, the Royal is not in confirm, and the Monarch will not travel through or complete its course of action on a region that is beyond the supervision of the opponent. The act of casting is not permitted if any of the tiles surrounding the Royal and the hitting rook were inhabited.

En Passant

When a pawn is moved two squares ahead from its initial position and an opposing pawn might have captured it had it moved only one square forward, the opposing pawn is immediately captured in a rare pawn capture. The advancing pawn is "passively" captured by the opponent "as it passes" the first square. If the piece had just advanced one square and the enemy pawn had taken normally, the position would have been the same. For the en passant capture to count, it must occur on the player's following turn, or the opportunity to do so would be lost. In this one and only circumstance, a seized component fails to relocate to the square of the captured piece.

Whenever a pawn advances to the opposite the participant's part of the surface, it gets elevated and can only be exchanged for an opponent's piece of a comparable color. These exchanges typically involve a princess, rook, a priest, or knight.

Promotion

Whenever a pawns advances to the opposite the participant's sector of the plane, it is advanced. When a different piece than the pawn is selected for promotion to the queen, this is known as underpromotion.Since the promoted piece might be any piece, including two queens, it is conceivable to have more of that type than at the beginning of the game.

Chapter 4

ESSENTIAL RULES AND GAMEPLAY

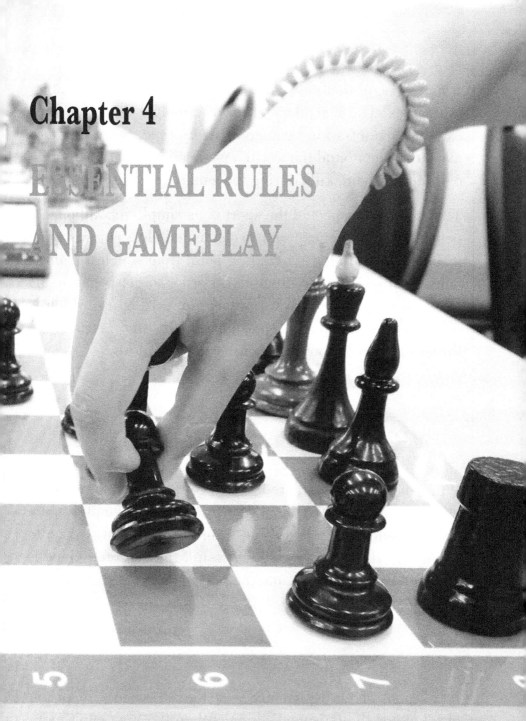

It may be said that chess is the most glamorous of all table-top games. The legendary clash of strategic minds ensures exciting, one-of-a-kind gameplay every time. Several grand-masters from around the world have been internationally recognized for their skills during the game's long history.

The appealing aspect of the sport is its simplicity: although a person with no prior experience can nonetheless enjoy playing it. It is crucial to have a starting point from which to launch oneself. Discover the essentials in order to get began using the easy-to-follow guide and ruleset for setting up, which is provided underneath. Then, spend some time learning all there is to know about the exciting game of chess.

4.1 Rules of the Game

White or other light-colored pieces go first and so on in a cyclical fashion between the players. Moving to an empty square is an option, but so is closing in on an opponent's piece to capture it. If the capture is successful, the captured piece is removed from the board, and the player who made the capture takes it.

Objective

In a game of chess, victory is achieved when one player checkmates the opponent's king. When the king can't move to any safe square, it's called checkmate. Even though the king is not under check, the game ends in a stalemate if there are no legal moves.

For checkmate to occur, the king must first be "in check," or vulnerable to capture by the opponent's piece. The king can then either move out of the check, or if that's not a possibility, use another piece to block check. During a match, the king may be in check multiple times with no apparent indication of who is winning.

The pieces in a chess game work together to accomplish tasks like capturing an opponent's piece or blocking an opponent's move. Sacrificing a pawn to create a blank row across the board, for example, might be used to "bait" the other player into a better strategic position.

The goal of most players is to dominate the board's middle. It will take a few moves to do this, as the row of pawns must be opened up for the other pieces to march forward. The rest of the game boils down to a choice: how to pursue the enemy king without giving up too many of your own pieces.

How Each Chess Piece Typically Moves

The basics of chess play are outlined here. genuinely are interested in playing a board game, you must be able to maneuver the components around on the surface of the board. Most chess grandmasters favor giving stronger abilities to pieces that can move about the board more easily.

The Mobility of Chess Pieces:

Rule of thumb for pawns is that they can only advance one square at a time. However, on their primary shift, they're provided with the option of moving two or three places forward. By moving ahead diagonally by a single square, the players are able to grab components from the adversary player.

PAWN • P

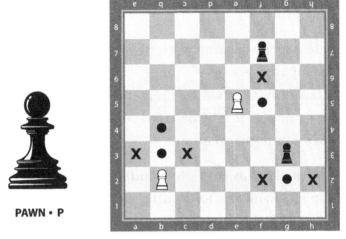

Rook: Rooks have the ability to move through a predetermined number of sectors in either the upward or downward direction.

ROOK • R

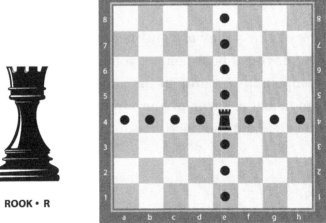

It's an L-shaped restriction for the two knights. That includes any permutation in which one square moves up and two move over, or vice versa.

KNIGHT · N

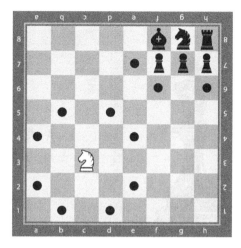

Bishop: Either of the two bishops can travel over an arbitrary number of diagonal squares.

BISHOP · B

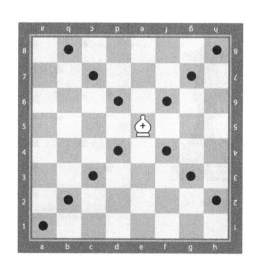

This allows it to shift an arbitrary number of squares in any combination of the x, y, and z directions.

Monarchs are capable of shifting a single area in any manner, nevertheless they have to repose following each movement they make. Monarchs can advance a single rectangle.

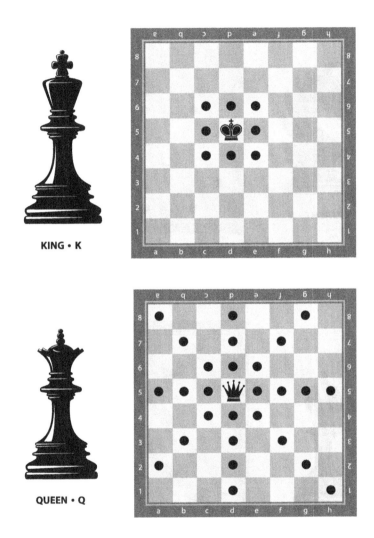

KING • K

QUEEN • Q

4.2 Standard Chess Regulations and Procedures

The Pawn Advancement Rule in Chess

Pawns can advance in rank according to the chess rulebook. Pawns can advance to higher positions on the board by using their unique abilities. However, the pawn cannot advance to the next position until it reaches the opposite side of the board.

It's not true that pawns can only be traded for captured pieces. The higher mobility of the queen makes it the preferred exchange for most pawns.

The Castling Rule of Chess

'castling' is a unique move in the rules of chess. You'll be able to accomplish two (2) major goals with this action. Find a secure location for the ruler, and then coax his rook from its retirement so it can participate in the battle.

You are only allowed to fortress whenever it is your opportunity to do this during the game of chess. The king shifts over two squares to one side, while the rook hops from a corner to a square near to the king. Castling, on the other hand, is permitted to take place given these particular conditions:

- It must be the king's first move.
- That rook's initial move is required.

- It is impossible for them to be any pawns, depending on knight or episcopal in the path connecting the sovereign and the other raven.
- You're going to no longer be able to fortress if your ruler is in checking or if your castle comes into checking during the game.

When a king is castled toward a certain side of the board, he ends up closer to that side. The term refers to this tactic in the game of chessboard. To "castle queenside" is to switch sides and advance to the other board. Every time the castling move is made, the king advances exactly two squares.

The chess equivalent of "Check" is "Checkmate."

In chess, checkmating your opponent's king is the ultimate goal. This happens only when the king is trapped and unable to flee. If a king cannot avoid checkmate, the game is ended.

- The king has three options to escape check according to the rules of the chessboard:
- Do something within the rules (other than castling) to move out of the path.
- Avoid the check by positioning another piece in its way.
- If your opponent's piece is in a position to threaten your king, capture it.

4.3 Etiquette and Sportsmanship in Chess

Chess may improve several aspects of one's character, including sportsmanship. The chess game, we hear from many parents, boosts their child's confidence. Others have told us that their child has learned sportsmanship through playing chess, especially how to gracefully handle setbacks and defeat.

Etiquette for tournaments is covered in our "Guide to Scholastic Tournaments" up top. In this section, which is relevant for club and tournament play, we go into greater detail regarding the subject. The following are some instances of both bad sportsmanship and rule-breaking.

Use proper etiquette and make a nice first impression. It's polite to shake hands with your rival before a match. For example, "Hello, I'm…" or "It's a pleasure to meet you, my name is…" are acceptable greetings.

Don't brag, insult, or try to bully your opponent. Some players use their ratings as a talking point, either to boast about their success or to try and put their opponents on the defensive.

Don't. Never mention anything that your rival could take the wrong way. Keep your expressions, body language, and gestures neutral.

Avoid engaging in debate with your rival. Ask the tournament director or someone in authority to issue a ruling if you and your opponent disagree about a move or if your opponent defies the rules and refuses to comply when asked to do so. This approach makes participants more likely to avoid expending unnecessary feelings while working out their differences.

Bring only the necessary supplies. No aids are allowed, such as paper or digital notes, tapes, or computers. (A Monroi or similar device to record plays is permitted by some tournament administrators.) Game forfeiture or time penalties may apply for infractions.

Don't offer or seek counsel. No one can give you direction on where to relocate. Also, if someone offers you advice, decline it. The tournament director should be contacted if someone tries to give advice.

Stop being so obnoxious. Talking to your opponent during a game is frowned upon and discouraged (with a few notable exceptions). Tapping a pencil or clicking chess pieces against the table, kicking the table, humming, singing, or talking to oneself are all other examples of unpleasant behavior. If your opponent refuses to stop doing any of these actions when asked, you should seek assistance from an adult or the tournament director.

Don't leave the game while it's going on. While your opponent is pondering a move, you are free to use the restroom, and in many tournaments, you can even watch games around you. Be wary of wasting too much of your time once your opponent has made a move. Don't swarm the other game's players or touch the table as you watch. Otherwise, you must leave a game in progress for an extended period with the approval of the tournament director. Make it apparent to your rival that you want to depart since you are resigning.

Keep everyone from knowing how you're doing in your game right now. It's not recommended to talk about or analyze your game near active games, even after it's finished. You should go to a calm area outside the game room.

Except for saying "check" (which is optional) or "checkmate," offering a draw, pointing out an unlawful move, or requesting a ruling from the tournament director, you may not speak to anybody else in the playing area.

Do not attempt to deceive your opponent by falsely announcing check, checkmate, or stalemate, gasping, or feigning dismay after making a terrible move.

Do not try to get the better of your opponent by shouting things like "hurry up!" or "go!" or "move!"

Chapter 5

BASIC OPENING PRINCIPLES

As the pawns slowly make their way across the board, the opening ranks begin to organize. On the battlefield, knights strike out to break up enemy ranks. Bishops, meantime, start looking for any opening in the enemy's defense so they can launch an attack and turn the game into a full-scale war.

Strategists start plotting their sophisticated schemes in the first game, patiently waiting for the right moment to launch them. The opening game is the first few moves of a chess game, during which pieces are produced and formations are assembled. That's because it's not meant to be extremely specific. There are no fixed boundaries between the different stages of a chess game, and the opening and middle game often blend into one another.

Since many high-level games are decided in the first few moves, chess openings have been studied more than any other aspect of the game. Even in the initial few moves, many crucial exchanges might occur. You can gain a positional and mental advantage over your opponent even if you aren't capturing their piece directly by disrupting their best-laid intentions.

Your opening plan can take any number of forms, just like any other phase of the game. There's no need to feel threatened, even if top-level players often study and recall dozens of moves worth of openings. While opening preparation is crucial at any skill level, it is just one phase of a much larger chess strategy. Just the initial few moves in a chess game can lead to an infinite number of outcomes. There are three primary types of openings that are considered to be the most solid from a strategic standpoint: the Flank Opening, the King's

Thank you from the bottom of my heart for choosing to read this book!

It is with immense gratitude that I address these words to you. It gives me enormous pleasure to know that you have decided to give your time and attention to these pages that I have written with commitment and dedication.

Creating this book has been an exciting journey, and my hope is that you have found it as enjoyable and inspiring to read as I have in writing it. Every word was carefully chosen with the goal of conveying a message, a story or a new perspective to you.

I am aware that you have a multitude of choices available to you when it comes to books, and the fact that you chose mine is a source of great pride and happiness. Your choice is invaluable to me, as it is the support and interest of readers like you that give meaning to my work as a writer.

If you have enjoyed the journey you have taken with these pages, I kindly ask you to **share your experience with others**. Reader reviews are a vital tool for raising awareness of a book and helping other readers make an informed choice.

If you feel inspired to do so, you might **take a few minutes to write a positive review** in which you could share your opinions. Even a few words can make a huge difference and help introduce the book to a wider audience.

Pawn Opening, and the Queen's Pawn Opening. Each of these three broad classes contains countless subclasses.

But we'll look at a couple of the most well-known variants and discuss what makes them work so well.

5.1 King's Pawn Openings

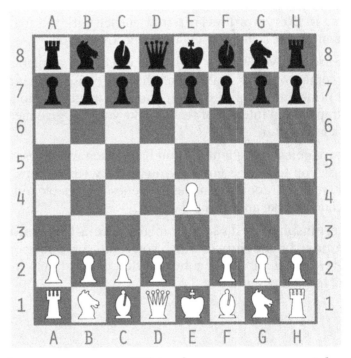

As early as move one, White has twenty potential opening movements, one of the most popular and effective being e4, the King's Pawn Opening. This may surprise inexperienced players, as it leaves the king's file wide open to attack. It was still difficult for Black to assault the king, especially if White used this time to strengthen their queen and bishop.

White's pawn travels to e4 to initiate the King's Pawn Opening. There, two stronger pieces can be sent out immediately.

The e4 opening is powerful because it quickly creates a position in the middle of the board and accelerates the development of the queen. While this leaves White's pawns vulnerable for the time being, it also presents an opportunity to quickly fortify the position with more instruments and stronger pieces.

How is Black supposed to respond to such a powerful introduction? The Sicilian Defense on c5 is the most popular choice in response to the King's Pawn Opening.

In chess, this is one of the most frequently seen opening moves. This example perfectly illustrates the differences between playing as White or Black by contrasting the strategies behind their opening moves.

Black's first move to c5 in the Sicilian Defense accomplishes little to develop pieces, in contrast to White's opening move to e4. However, in addition to these significant advantages, there are many others.

Since White has the initiative by default, Black has a tough time catching up and often ends up in a losing position. The King's Pawn Opening is White's first move, emphasizing fast domination and executing a plan. In contrast, the Sicilian Defense is a more cautious response. While White can quickly acquire control of the kingside files, Black has the advantage of a strong phalanx of pawns on the queenside field. Quick action on Blacks will allow them to create and fortify their control zone against Whites' assault.

As an alternative, Black could play the even more conservative Caro-Kann Defense, in which the pawn advances only one square to c6. More strategic players, looking to gain a long-term positional advantage and less concerned with initiating exchanges, tend to favor this approach.

Some players, of course, favor head-on conflict. The King's Pawn Opening can be met with e5 or an Open Game if you prefer a more dynamic style of play. The most typical response to White's Nf3, which threatens Black's pawn, is Nc6.

As mentioned earlier in Lopez's opening, both players must react fast and decisively in the Ruy.

The beautiful thing about Ruy Lopez is that every position in the game has multiple viable options for both players. In contrast to more mechanical techniques, the Ruy Lopez gives astute tacticians a full feast of attacks and gambits to pursue. This opening is one of the most researched phenomena in chess due to the wide variety of play chains that can develop from it.

Although King's Pawn Openings are the most popular, that doesn't mean there aren't other strong options. Although it is less common, opening the pawn on the queen's file has certain benefits.

5.2 Queen's Pawn Opening

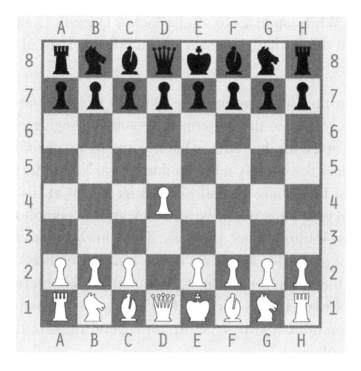

Similar to the King's Pawn Opening, the goal of this opening is to quickly establish dominance in the middle of the board. By outlet on d4, White sets himself up to accomplish the more difficult queenside castling and develop his bishop on the queenside.

When Black plays d5, a common continuation of this opening is for White to offer the Queen's Gambit by advancing another pawn to c4. Black must now make a difficult choice. By taking the offered pawn with dxc4, they risk giving White complete control of the middle game. On the opposite conjunction, in the event that Black refuses to take the offer of food, White has the ability to take advantage of themselves.

Above, White appears to offer Black a Queen's Gambit. Token, but the exchange comes with a poisoned gift of a tough decision.

Early in the 20th century, the Queen's Gambit was played frequently, but as the hypermodern school progressed, more players opted for the Indian Defense and its variants. Instead, Black uses the slightly non-standard move Nf6 in the opening round of this plan. Instead of meeting White at his door or trying to create his power base, Black spins a complex web to sabotage White's "free" progress. The Nimzo-Indian Defense is one of many developments of the Indian Defense, and it is among the strongest and most frequently encountered at all levels of play. In this variant, Black chooses to postpone the formation of his pawn structure for several turns to throw off White's plans.

Knowing they would have to sacrifice their kingside bishop eventually, Black in the Nimzo-Indian Defense rushes to deploy it.

There are always alternatives to the King and Queen's Pawn Openings, even though their strength lies in gaining a dominant position in the center. The third and final major class of openings is the Flank opening, designed to undermine central authority.

5.3 Flanking Holes

The Flank openings are a nod to military flanking movements, in which one force avoids the center of the board and instead threatens from the sides. Several other opening movements could be classified as Flank, but 1.Nf3 and 1.c4 are the most popular.

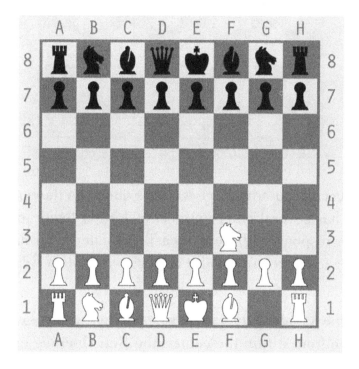

The English Opening is a common name for the easier of the two entrances, 1.c4.

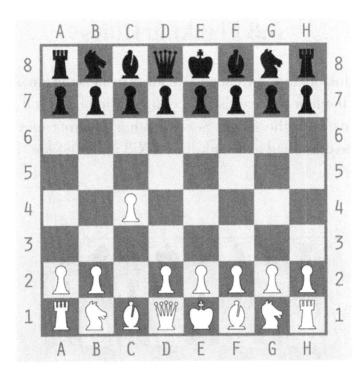

White has a clear advantage with the queen on the board, but he also has several other options, making it tough for Black to find a response. White can easily threaten both flanks by reverting to a Queen's Gambit or advancing into a Réti Opening.

Unlike the King's or Queen's pawn openings, which exert their influence from within the center, the Réti Opening exerts its influence from the outside. The Réti Opening is a common continuation of the Zukertort Opening, the moniker for 1.Nf3. This opening is a classic illustration of the hypermodern school of strategy, similar to the Indian Defenses in that both rely heavily on the rapid deployment of knights. Hypermodern players are more likely to employ fluid strategies than their classical counterparts, who choose a more tactical approach to the game. They believe that the center of the board is a valuable strategic asset but that it is best controlled by external threats rather than direct conflict, as demonstrated by the Réti Opening.

5.4 Choosing Your Opening

You're well-versed in 1.e4, 1.d4, 1.c4, and 1.Nf3, the four most common opening moves. You have also gained knowledge on how to progress the game from these gaps, whether you are Black or White. While many grandmasters have speculated as to which of these approaches is the most effective, the truth is that there is no one set of moves that would guarantee victory in every game. If such were the case, chess as a hobby would die out.

Whether opening is "strongest" is less important than figuring out which outlets work best with your playing style. Do you like more succinct games that rely heavily on tactical skills? You may succeed with the King's Pawn Openings, while the Queen's Pawn Openings and Queen's Gambit are useful for players who value flexibility and conflict.

Alternatively, the Flank openings may be the most fun if you prefer to outmaneuver and out scheming your opponents.

If you've gathered sufficient knowledge, you ought to extend some consideration to your rival. If your opponent has you beat in raw tactics, you might want a more organized opening to solidify your strategy before you fight. On the other hand, you could foil a cunning tactician's complex tactics by launching a devastating, frontal attack. Maintain a state of constant confusion and unpredictability for the other person on all occasions. The initial few movements of the opening sequence could potentially spark off an upward spiral that has repercussions throughout the remainder of the competition. But don't think you've lost the war because you lost the first fight.

Similarly, you should never relax your guard because you believe your initial moves were successful. A few well-placed movements can completely alter the course of a chess game. The middle game is the least explored area of chess strategy, in contrast to the openings and the endgames. In games of chess it is important to remember that even the minutest of minutiae can have a significant impact on the game. Keep these opening ideas in mind as you go on and think about how they can shape your game in the after-major play period.

Chapter 6

BASIC TACTICS

Chess is built on a foundation of tactics, so the entire game goes down with them when they fail. Tactical errors are more common among novices, although even the best players occasionally misplace pieces. In the first few dozen games, World Champions made tactical errors that cost them the match moves. Some games have been lost by international grandmasters in as few as six moves. Considering that the people who follow me are human and not chess-playing computers, it makes sense that we will continually experience tactical setbacks. Experienced players rarely leave a piece hanging, allowing for a one-pass capture. Such blunders are rare and usually don't teach us anything useful. It's usually due to technical pitfalls or negligence when a player loses an asset in more than one movement. Expect double assaults and lost opportunities to report them. Let's start with some rookie mistakes and catch some pros in their own nets.

6.1 How to Choose the Right Openings

Strategic planning constitutes the vast majority of a chess game. If the renowned claim is true for the master, then it must be even more so for the novice and club player. Improving your tactical skills is the greatest and most successful way to increase your chess efficiency because it allows you to recognize the common mating patterns and material-winning tactical motifs that are so crucial to the outcome of a game. Without a doubt, the best method to develop excellent tactical vision is to perform drills that teach you to recognize the tactical components that comprise every composition. This book examines the essential chess positions that every player should master. The importance of learning the fundamentals of strategy before attempting anything more complex cannot be overstated.

Improve your chess skills by drilling the tried-and-true strategies. Gain an edge in your next game by brushing up on the fundamentals of chess strategy, learning several classic openings, and understanding some important endgame principles.

Playing rudimentary chess instead of trying to memorize all those theoretical lines is the correct choice for a novice.

Not all opportunities are suitable for novices in the same way they are for experts.

Many passages necessitate an in-depth familiarity with complex strategic theories and the nuanced ordering of movements. First, keep these five opening ideas in mind at all times:

* Assume command of the hub. (Most notably the squares e4, d4, e5, and d5)
* Create pieces that will actively threaten your opponent's.
* Third, avoid relocating the same piece twice if at all possible.
* A rim-based knight is an idiot, (The flexibility and range of your components will expand dramatically as you work towards the center.)

- Fifth, make sure your King is secure. (You put your King in a very vulnerable position if you leave him in the middle.)

Once we're comfortable with these fundamental chess opening principles, we can look for good chess openings for beginners.

The best chess starts for beginners include the qualities that follow:

- It's easy to get yourself set up and you can start playing instantaneously without any training.
- based on fundamental concepts rather than a dry recitation of doctrine.
- it promotes a peaceful stalemate.

6.2 Double Attack

A Double Attack is when two threats are established versus a player after a single move in chess. In addition, if this move creates threats where the same piece attacks two enemy pieces, All forks are double assaults, but not all double attacks are forks.

Pieces can be captured without the double attack producing any particularly dangerous dangers. Among the various forms of trouble are:

- Threatening Parts

- Squares under attack
- A checkmate threat

Double-Attack Techniques

Identifying double attack openings is the first step in exploiting them. The ability to spot pieces that aren't being defended and take out the defenses of lesser fragments with only one defender is the most important to hone. This will help you find holes in your opponent's defenses, allowing you to launch simultaneous attacks on multiple pieces.

Training your board awareness is essential. Playing games for extended periods will help you improve. Whenever performing Speedy Chess, it is going to be tough to determine a moment to fully analyze the board and uncover these shortcomings. This will make it challenging.

6.3 Discovered Attacks

In chess, a found attack is when one piece's movement enables an attack on another piece. Some of the most devastating chess moves are those that are discovered attacks. They're so common in practice that the "discovered check" can be treated as a separate field of inquiry.

As the piece being moved has the option to attack as well, the detected attack becomes a very devastating double strike.

What Role Do Discovered Attacks Play?

Discovered attacks, like other sorts of double attacks, are particularly effective since the defense is often unable to deal with two threats at once. In most cases, this approach will lead to the aggressor being awarded an amount of material benefit following every single one of the moves that they have done.

In most cases, the success of a detected attack depends on:

1. a weak king. The idea is that your opponent will have to cope with the threat you've generated by putting the king in check.

2. A piece with no defenses. This is the weak spot that you've identified as an attacker. While your opponent is preoccupied with defending their king, you can easily take their unguarded piece.

The discovered check is one type of discovered attack, but there are others as well. Even if an attack is thwarted without any loot being taken, it may still be useful. You gain a tempo even if you don't capture anything because your opponent will have to spend a turn relocating her pieces out of your way.

However, the difficulty of anticipating a detected attack is another reason they could be so devastating. Any piece can be used to initiate a detected attack, unlike skewers and pins which require specific ones.

6.4 Skewers and Hooks

A chess player has a wide array of tools at his disposal. The skewer and pin is a devastating attack that targets both the target piece and the piece directly behind it. Players are able to achieve this goal by attacking a king from his or her rear position. To reveal the hidden element, the king must be moved. When a piece in front of the king is pinned, the king is pinned as well, making it impossible for the piece to move out of harm's way.

You won't often find your chess opponent giving you simple skewers or pins that leave some of his strongest pieces hanging. Instead, a chess player must be well-versed in the use of various methods for setting up skewers and pins. These tips can help you become the dominant player in a game you once thought was out of your reach.

STRATEGIC PLANNING AND POSITIONAL UNDERSTANDING

The term "positional play" (or "positional style") appears frequently in chess discussions. Gaining an advantageous position while weakening your opponent's is the goal of positional play. Gaining a beneficial vantage point improves your offensive and strategic options. Even though he could recognize tactical combinations and world champion Alexander Alekhine, Rudolph Spielmann of the early 20th century complained that he could never get Alekhine's positions.

7.1 Position Evaluation

You need to assess a situation and establish who has the upper hand before you can work to improve your position. The ability to evaluate functions accurately cannot be picked up overnight but developed and honed throughout a player's chess career. Simple assessments are a good place to start, and you may progress to more nuanced ones as you learn more via practice and experimentation.

Material

Counting the points of the pieces on both sides is the quickest and easiest approach to judging a position's strength. A side with five additional details usually wins, and even a rookie can see this just by looking at the place. A material imbalance, in which one side has a knight and bishop while the other just has a rook and pawn, can make a position difficult to evaluate. Both are worth six points, but knowing which

Thank you from the bottom of my heart for choosing to read this book!

It is with immense gratitude that I address these words to you. It gives me enormous pleasure to know that you have decided to give your time and attention to these pages that I have written with commitment and dedication.

Creating this book has been an exciting journey, and my hope is that you have found it as enjoyable and inspiring to read as I have in writing it. Every word was carefully chosen with the goal of conveying a message, a story or a new perspective to you.

I am aware that you have a multitude of choices available to you when it comes to books, and the fact that you chose mine is a source of great pride and happiness. Your choice is invaluable to me, as it is the support and interest of readers like you that give meaning to my work as a writer.

If you have enjoyed the journey you have taken with these pages, I kindly ask you to **share your experience with others**. Reader reviews are a vital tool for raising awareness of a book and helping other readers make an informed choice.

If you feel inspired to do so, you might **take a few minutes to write a positive review** in which you could share your opinions. Even a few words can make a huge difference and help introduce the book to a wider audience.

is preferable in a given situation is a skill that can only be honed with practice.

Space

If both players are equally skilled, the one who controls more territory has a slight edge. The amount of space a player has is equal to the amount of settlement in their half of the board that is uncontested by the opposing player's pieces.

To begin, let's tally up the territory that White currently occupies. To do this, visualize a line down the middle of the board, separating the white side from the black side. One point will be awarded to White for each piece in Black's half of the board, and one point will be awarded for each square in Black's half that White has guarded or attacked. A point bonus will be awarded for each additional piece that controls a square. Here's how White's dominance on the board manifests itself.

White's overall spatial dominance is 16. While the pawn on c4 and the knight on c3 both have access to b5, the bishop on e2 controls the square because the e2 bishop would protect the c4 instrument if it captured a black piece there. Let's do that with black, too.

With the f6 knight pinned and unable to move without exposing the black queen, Black only controls 6 of the 8 available squares. Therefore, white has a considerable spatial advantage at the moment. More board space gives you an edge over your opponent because your pieces can move freely while theirs are crowded together. If the board is larger, you'll have more room to maneuver your leftovers into an attacking position, while your opponent will be forced to move more slowly.

In-Game Action

Having well-placed, active, and coordinated pieces can give you a significant positional advantage. You want your knights guarding the center, your bishops controlling the diagonals, and your rooks on the open file. Pieces that are well coordinated don't interfere with one another but enhance one another, provide mutual defense, and avoid vulnerable open squares.

White has excellent placement here, controlling numerous squares deep within the Black's base. The bishops hold control of the diagonals, and the rooks have broken through to the seventh rank via the open file. In contrast, Black's pieces are imprisoned in their base. White has a decisive piece activity advantage at the moment.

Central Control

Gaining a strategic edge often requires battling for control of the center. When you dominate the center of the board, your pieces can freely move from one side to the other, giving you a significant advantage in both space and piece activity, while your opponent's pieces may find themselves trapped on one side of the board.

Above, the four most crucial core squares—e4, d4, e5, and d5—are indicated by the dots. Centering on the crosses, you can see how far out from it you really are. In chess, the goal is to keep as many of your pieces in the four center squares as possible, forcing your opponent's pieces to retreat or trade if they threaten your dominance.

Black's pieces aren't very well placed to contest white's central supremacy, while whites are in an ideal position to control the center. Thus, white has the space and piece activity advantage, and his pieces can move freely to either side of the board, whereas black's pieces, for example, have a tough time getting from a6 to the kingside.

Pawn Arrangement

The condition of each player's pawn structure is also a major consideration when assessing a position. The less solitary, backward, and doubled pawns there are in a player's pawn structure, the stronger that structure is considered to be.

While Black only has two pawn islands, White has three. Having fewer pawn islands is preferable, so this counts against White. White has a lone piece on a5 and pawns moving in the other direction on c3. Black has pawn on a6 and a pawn facing the wrong way on h6. Black has an extra instrument in the center of the board, which might be useful because it gives Black greater centralized control. Black has the better pawn structure.

Watching the pawn structure is often a useful indicator of the optimal plan in chess. If Black attempted to move in the position shown above, he would attempt to capture the vulnerable white pawn located on c3. Black can play...Rc4 followed by...Rec8 to double rooks and launch a frontal assault on this position. Black might potentially attack White's lone a-pawn from behind by moving a rook from c4 to a4.

Safety King

If your king is vulnerable, all other advantages you may have will be rendered useless. The security of your king is of utmost significance, and if yours is the safer option, you'll be in a better position to seize the initiative and launch attacks without fear of being checkmated.

Here, white's king is well-protected by a barrier of pawns and other pieces, while the Black's is in a precarious position. The black king is quite susceptible, thus black always has to be on the alert for threats like the white bishop going to h6, the white rook coming, and so on.

After the queens have been traded, the king usually feels much more secure. This trend continues as the game progresses. Since the king usually plays an active role in the endgame, king activity, rather than king safety, is more significant in judging a position at that stage of the game; however, we shall examine this topic in greater depth in a subsequent tutorial.

Chapter 8

ENDGAME TACTICS

This is your last chance to demonstrate your skills as a chess player. To avoid relying too heavily on endgame tactics, most players want to outplay their opponents in the middlegame.

However, these players usually fall short in the endgame since mastering the endgame technique requires considerable time and effort. Even more so when playing against opponents of the same or greater skill, knowing the method is crucial.

You should know the fundamentals of the endgame as a beginner. Here's a rundown of each:

A passed pawn can't be blocked by an opponent's means because there are no other pawns on the same file or the files next to it.

Pawn's square: A fictitious square where the king can retake a passed pawn.

If you start with the pawn and draw a diagonal to the rear rank, you'll end up with the pawn's square.

If it were Black's turn, he could play Ke4 to invade the pawn's square and checkmate the advancing piece. However, if White has the initiative, he can advance the pawn because Black's king cannot reach it in time.

Triangulation is a strategy that maintains contact with the opponent yet "passes" their move. The closest analogy in chess would be this. Here's an illustration:

Now White gets to make a move. For instance, Black can achieve a stalemate position if White directly promotes the c-pawn. To begin, 1.Kd5, Kc8 2.Kd6, Kc8 3.c7+, Kc8 4.Kc6=.

Instead, White resorts to triangulation in order to "lose a move," as if Black were to play, White would play Kb6, winning the a-pawn, and Black would be unable to checkmate the white king. White comfortably wins after 1.Kd5, Kc8 2.Kc4!, Kb8 3.Kc4!, Kc7.

King-made "Zugzwang" formation, where two kings face each other across an odd-numbered square diagonal.

White can "gain the opposition" by playing Ke4, which will force Black to make a lateral or retreating move. If White places Ke1 in his spot on the right, he is considered to have won the game. Nevertheless, the idea of "diagonal opposition," which is mentioned in the introduction, is not going to be covered here. Shouldering is a king move that causes the adversary king to retreat off the board. Shouldering occurs as a result of repeated use of opposition.

When a bishop is the wrong color, it cannot promote a passed rook pawn, and the game is drawn 90% of the time.

Black can practically ensure a draw if it retains the king and the green squares in the following diagram. Take note of the contrasting colors of the bishop's square (d3) and the pawn's promotion square (h8).

Here's how you can come out on top in case you're interested: You arrange the bishop and pawn in this way. For White to win, his king must be in close enough proximity to Black's king, bishop, and pawn to "shoulder" the latter away from the pawn.

8.1 Endgame Tactics and Moves

Your careful planning and forethought will pay off when the endgame finally arrives. If you want to be able to shout like the Persians, here are some suggestions to help you reach that last round: Checkmate!

Plan your next steps: You might believe this is more of a middlegame concern, but tiny piece calculation is crucial at any stage. This is an ever-present facet of your chess game, encompassing both subtle and radical modifications. There is no end to planning and executing strategies.

Bring out the king: The king can threaten pawns and protect other pieces, but he may be better off where he is if there are many other pieces on the board.

Take cautious when making rook exchanges: Keep in mind that a draw is common after a rook exchange. Take this option seriously.

Don't let your pawns become scattered: If at all possible, try to avoid having pawns that are paired up or all by themselves. This can be avoided in the endgame with careful preparation in the middlegame or even the opener.

Play aggressively, yet strategically: Take the king as far forward as you can while still allowing the pawns to advance.

Pawns speed up the game since they can be substituted with other pieces when necessary. A "dead move" occurs when two kings face each other and one of them moves, causing the other to lose territory.

Learn to hold your cards close and when to play your hand: While it's possible to make advantageous piece exchanges in the endgame, it's crucial to keep your pawns till then.

There are two sides to the board, and it's beneficial to make advantage of both of them. If you do this, your opponent may have trouble defending both flanks, giving you an opportunity to promote one of your pawns. The rook's solidity is something to rely on. A passed pawn gains support from a rook behind it, allowing it to continue its advance. When an enemy king is in the way of a pawn, the rook can provide lateral support. Both the rook and the pawn can help you win the game. Any chivalry buffs out there?

In an open position, the bishop is considered the stronger piece. The knight is the superior piece in a closed position. Open diagonals make it simpler for the bishop to move, and a knight can easily leap over a row of locked pawns. All of your preparation and planning will pay off in the endgame, when you have the opportunity to checkmate your opponent's king.

The Final Game: How to Get Better?

You can improve your chess game at any skill level. And if you take the appropriate approach and form positive routines, success will come easily and quickly. Learning the rules, playing many games, analyzing your play, solving problems, studying the endgames, skipping the openings, and double-checking your moves are all necessary for improvement.

Be Aware of the Regulations

It makes no difference whether you are completely confident in your understanding of the game's rules or whether you believe you have mastered them. It is always smart to study the moves of the pieces as well as the special rules that are exclusive to chess, even if you are already an accomplished chess player. The fundamental guidelines and tactics can be found in this section.

Play More Games

Chess is not an exception to the rule that you cannot get better at something if you do not put in as much effort as you can over a period of time. Make the most of every opportunity you have to compete in a game, whether it be away from home, on your computer, or at home.

Exercise Your Chess Skills

The definition of a tactic is a small miniature problem that needs to be solved. They provide a realistic simulation of scenarios in which you stand a chance of success. It's like playing chess, but instead of starting at the beginning, you go straight to the exciting part where you're already winning!

Resolve free puzzles.

Most chess matches don't end quickly, which comes as a bit of a surprise. After many turns have been played and most of the players have been transferred, the winner is declared. In many cases, the only pieces and pawns that are left on the chessboard are the kings and a few other random pieces.

This is the so-called "final," in which your objective will typically be to raise one of your pawns to a higher rank, such as a queen, in the chess game. Mastering the endgames will put you in a better position to win a lot of games.

You'll have the opportunity to hone your skills by practicing some of the most typical endings right here.

Do Not Waste Time Storing Openings

The so-called "openings" are tedious sequences of movements, but many chess players make the rookie mistake of wasting their time by trying to memorize them. The majority of your opponents are likely to be unfamiliar with many openings, and even if they are familiar with some beginnings, the likelihood that they will play along the lines of the game that you have studied is still quite low. This is the dilemma.

Chapter 9

CHESS MINDSET:
DEVELOPING THE RIGHT
MENTAL ATTITUDE

The mental game is crucial in chess. Focus and mental readiness are required. Keeping your emotions in check and keeping your eye on the big picture can mean the difference between winning and losing a game. Challenges with self-motivation, error-correction, and letting go reflect broader issues with personal growth.

Mastery of one's own mind and willpower are just as important as natural ability in the game of chess. Being a good chess player requires involve more than just memorizing moves and strategies.

1. Mental Preparation is Critical

The top chess players get started playing right away. Chess needs complete focus. The secret to success is having mental toughness before the game. While there are countless ways in which players get ready, maintaining attention and focus is a common objective. Chess is a powerful tool for switching your attention from issues and irritations to something else.

2. Calmness is a Virtue

One of the most valuable traits in a chess player is tolerance. A chess game frequently goes on for more than 30 minutes. It may not seem like much, but it takes more than 30 minutes of total focus. Players must remain patient and use reason during this period. You shouldn't try to win a game in record time. Instead, engage in the activity and consider your options to avoid disappointing errors.

3. Keep the board's big vision in the forefront of your mind at all times.

A competent chess player needs to think about the subsequent moves to make a move. Chess requires considerable thought, and moving a piece without considering how it may affect the entire game sets you up to lose. Good chess players are familiar with every piece on the board and can anticipate their opponent's moves as they pick which piece and how to play it.

4. When playing chess, control your emotions.

Being able to manage your emotions will improve your game. During a game, a player goes through a wide range of emotions. Your prospects of defeating your opponent are ruined if you let your emotions rule you. Whether you are disappointed, excited, upset with yourself, or frustrated shouldn't matter when playing. Just take an inhalation or two and perform normally again.

5. Never Undervalue Your Chess Rival

Learn to play your best regardless of who your opponent is by challenging yourself to have a consistent mindset. Every game should present a difficult test for the players. It is improper to take it easy even when one's opponent is a higher-ranked player than oneself because doing so encourages carelessness.

6. Believe In Yourself

Playing a more skilled opponent does not guarantee losing the game. Even newbies outperform experts. Enter the game believing you have an equal chance of winning. Pay close attention to every action and maximize the chance to gain knowledge.

7. Avoid Allowing Surprises to Destroy Your Chess Game

It is highly unpleasant when your adversary shocks you with an unexpected move. Mentally get yourself ready for this. You must remain calm and keep your focus if you are taken by surprise. Practice refocusing and maintaining your concentration. Avoid overreacting or acting aggressively.

8. Stay Motivated

Self-talk that encourages and inspires you is crucial in chess and in life. The outcome of the game is determined by our internal monologue. The benefits of thinking negatively are nothing. If you're always down on yourself during the game, it'll be hard to focus. Keep yourself inspired, remember the lessons you've learned, and revel in your successes as they happen.

9. Learn to Play Chess While Handling Distractions

Distractions will be present regardless of whether you play face-to-face or online. Try not to let anger consume you. Take a deep breath and let the distraction pass. If you're having trouble ignoring distractions, try zeroing down on the task at hand.

10. Learn From Past Chess Mistakes

Making an error in a chess game can be upsetting and demotivating. It is important to keep this from affecting the rest of your game or tournaments you play, but take note of the mistake and never make it again. One mistake should only ruin part of the game, put the error out of your mind during the game and analyze it afterward.

11. Dedication Creates Chess Champions

One of chess's many benefits is that individual practice is possible. It is possible to work on plans in advance and be ready to deal with the game your opponent plays, in addition to the wealth of information available online. Winners are made through dedicated practice.

12. Embrace The Good in a Chess Competition

Competition is healthy, despite the fact that it can be stressful at times. It gives gamers the opportunity to uncover their latent potential and practice newly acquired abilities. Players will also have the opportunity to feel the satisfaction of practicing and winning as a result of participating in the tournament. Learning how to deal with the competitive nature of chess is an excellent method to develop one's life skills because many of the obstacles encountered in a game of chess are relevant to real life.

Chapter 10

READING THE OPPONENT: UNDERSTANDING STRATEGIES AND PATTERN

ASSIMILATION OF ACTIVE PIECES

It needs to be more to view the pieces as they are on the board to win a game of chess. Additionally, you must be able to visualize possibilities and threats for both your pieces and your adversary's. In this practice, we'll learn some fundamental visualization skills for the active pieces on the board.

Imagine you want to relocate your Bishop. You must see the active pieces on the board before finding a safe tile to move your Bishop.

It's your turn in the illustration below if you're playing White. A simple move by your Bishop can remove another piece in only one move. Can you picture in your mind's eye an arrow that will lead to the Bishop depicted below, capturing an adversary's piece? If it helps, use your finger to make a line connecting the active piece to the highlighted Bishop.

You were right if you imagined a straight line between the White Bishop and the Black Bishop.

See the picture below.

When you turn to move, picture yourself stealing an enemy piece.

If you are able to capture a piece from your rival without losing anything yourself, you ought to perform so. However, you must consciously picture where your pieces can go and, more significantly, whether they can move to a square that captures an opponent's piece to recognize that you have a chance in the first place.

As you get better, you can picture these arrows without using your finger to make a point. But if you start by pointing first, we guarantee you'll pick things up more quickly.

Let's try another illustration. In the picture below, the highlighted Rook has the chance to capture an enemy piece. Can you see the Rook's path to capture the enemy piece?

You successfully visualized if you imagined a line connecting the Black Knight and the Rook. See the picture below.

Those were simple. Try a more difficult one. A bishop that can take another piece in one move is seen in the figure below. Then, picture the Bishop capturing the adversary's piece. Once you are prepared for the solution, turn to the following page.

In chess slang, the Bishop pointing toward the Rook in the other corner is known as being fianchettoed. A bishop is fianchettoed when it is moved toward the flank to control the long diagonal across the board.

In this situation, many novice players lose their Rook because they cannot recognize an enemy Bishop. In a real game, you would win handily if you saw this play.

ESTIMATING THE INTENTIONS OF YOUR ENEMIES

You can now approximately determine which pieces are active and see when one of your pieces may attack another. Your opponent's movements, however, are only one aspect of the game. Additionally, you need to see and understand when your adversary has the potential to strike you.

We may assume your opponent wants to win the game just as much as you do. Your opponent's primary goal at the first level will be to remove your pieces or checkmate you.

Your opponent may attempt to perform one of those two things every time they move. You must thus think about your opponent's active pieces each time they move.

For instance, Black recently created the Bishop in the figure below. Imagine the item that was highlighted. What do you suppose Black's strategy with his Bishop is?

Black would have attempted to harm your White Knight if you had foreseen it. You're correct. View the illustration below.

You must imagine and anticipate your opponent's movements as if you were using their pieces whenever they make a move. What would be my best move using my opponent's pieces? You should anticipate your opponent's finest movements so that you may be ready for them in advance. You shouldn't assume your opponent won't notice when you make a successful move. Be ready for your adversary to make the best move possible.

Keep openings in mind.

We discussed different chess openings in the earlier chapters of this book, as well as some of their benefits and drawbacks. Did you realize the majority of competitors in tournaments use these openings? Knowing this makes it smart to memorize these opportunities to anticipate how your opponent will choose to build their offense. This will provide you with a wealth of tactics for choosing to play defensively or offensively.

Analyse the actions of your adversary.

Do not react promptly to an action made by your opponent. Analyze and comprehend the reasoning behind your opponent's initial move. You can plan your following movements after evaluating his action to better understand his approach. This advice makes more sense, especially early in the game. Simply analyzing your opponent's opening can help you determine his playing style. This can also assist you in recognizing any potential dangers your adversary may have in store for you, allowing you to respond appropriately.

Make the best move.

There may occasionally be more than one smart move. Know which action is the greatest choice for you. Analyze the benefits and drawbacks of each possibility and pick the one that works most effectively with you. In order to decide what steps to take, you could discover it helpful to ask yourself outlined below:

- Can you think of any more steps that will facilitate your move?
- To a better square, your piece?

- Would you choose a different piece to move to improve your position?
- Will this move enable you to properly counter your opponent's threat?
- Will the piece you decide to move with this move be in a safe square?
- The optimal course of action is the decision that provides satisfactory answers to the questions mentioned earlier. Decide on that move, then execute it.

Establish a plan.

Chess victory does not come from making haphazard moves and hoping for good fortune. For every step you make, you must have a strategy in place. There is a connection between everything you do. You may create a strategy using the ideas behind chess openings.

Another crucial thing to remember is to limit switching between several plans within a single game. You will lose clarity if you continually change your mind, which might favor your adversary. Consequently, make a plan and follow it.

You must comprehend the value of your pieces at various game phases if you want to know how much they are worth. Don't exchange valuable items for less valuable ones. Before making any move, consider the piece's value and the ramifications of losing a piece.

Properly and quickly develop.

You must develop your pieces early in the game while the clock runs. In the event that you neglect to take utilization of the scenario, your opponent will hit you with force if they get the opportunity. Focusing on improving our pawns is a mistake most of us make when we are still beginners. Even while pawn formation and development are crucial, we tend to pay less attention to the other pieces when we solely concentrate on moving the pawns forward.

More than a group of pawns positioned in the game's center, the other significant pieces decide your place. Therefore, be careful to develop your crucial parts as quickly as feasible. Remember that you should only create a piece if it makes sense. Always have a purpose for developing any piece on the board and know that it will only help you if you develop a piece with a worthy cause.

Recognize when to trade.

Keeping all pieces on the board is not the key to winning a game. Knowing when to lose any piece on the board is important. Ensure you only exchange your pieces at the appropriate moments to avoid losing a piece and obtaining a crucial piece from your opponent. Before you trade, bear the following advice in mind:

Don't swap anything out except doing so will improve your standing among competitors. This becomes of utmost importance when there are a handful of pieces left on the board among the two opponents. Avoid exchanging when your opponent's squares are constrained and offer little room for piece development. You will receive no profit from the trade. Never make an exchange if you are aware that your opponent has more pieces than you have; doing so will only make matters worse.

Always be on guard.

Never relax because of one successful move alone. Only when the game is over can you afford to relax your guard. Until then, you must be vigilant, watch for threats from your foe, and take appropriate action. Your competitor only needs yourself to commit at least a single oversight for them to establish a major advantage over you. So, always be on guard.

Never take risks you shouldn't.

While playing aggressively can help you, unthinkingly can hurt your chances of winning. Never take unwarranted chances that could lose you the victory. Do not take unplanned risks.

Avoid writing supplemental checks.

Giving a check will put your opponent on edge but be sure there is a reason for each one. By delivering checks that are completely unnecessary, you are not only squandering your own precious time but also the time of your attacker. If you chose your actions carefully, you could use that time more. Never write a cheque for no reason.

Checkmate and Check

Beginners need to know the distinction between these two terminologies. "Check" and "checkmate" are not the same thing. These are two distinct concepts that should be used in various ways. It is claimed that the checked is required because a checkmate can occur.

You check whether a competitor's monarch is in danger. It's possible the king will relocate now that he's acknowledged your ultimatum. If you use the expression "check," your opponent will know something is up. The monarch now resides in an unsafe environment and must be moved. Most newcomers will look past this option and instead try to capture the enemy king. The truth is that your enemy needs to be made aware of any danger before it can be effectively countered. The enemy subsequently needs to prepare to conceal its king.

A checkmate, on the other hand, means the game is over. No matter where he is relocated, the monarch is constantly in peril. It indicates that we've reached the final score. Saying the word you've lost the competition..

Don't get bored and ruin your chess game!

Chess is a fascinating yet difficult game. There is an extensive education trajectory, so newcomers should be ready to lose and should plan for stalemate situations when they do. Fascinating and useful tactics, such as Sicilian protection, can be learned with time and effort. There are six ways for a chess game to conclude in a draw: perpetual check, insufficient mating material, repetition of movements, fifty-move rule, draw by agreement, and last but not least, the stalemate, which is the one that will be our main topic in this section.

Under a chess stalemate, the king is not under check, and the player is unable to make a move that would be legal. The chess game concludes in a draw when there is a stalemate. Stalemate is a draw in standard chess. However, stalemate is not regarded as a draw in some historical and contemporary chess variations.

The player who brings a game of Shatranj, similar to chess, to a deadlock is declared the winner. Even in this day and age, a lot of individuals have advocated to reinstate this restriction. Remember that the player's likelihood of drawing a game while in a losing position is quite slim. Only if the adversary is not paying attention to your next actions can a standstill be achieved.

Reasons Why Negotiations Stalled

The response is bland. It would be in your best interests to try and force a draw when you cannot win, and your opponent has the upper hand.

There are various techniques to force a tie in a game, including: Putting your king in a fixed position so it cannot move. Then offer all of your other pieces in a way that forces them to be taken. Next, BOOM!

You've reached a deadlock, and the match is a draw. Additionally, if there are no pieces left in the game other than the two kings and one pawn, you can end the game using the straightforward method shown below. If you were the black player, try the following scenario and learn to always conclude the game in a draw.

Now, if you are sitting across from your opponent, you must be trying to prevent reaching a deadlock. There is only one way to do this: after making your next move, check to determine if your opponent's king or other chess piece can still move.

CONCLUSION

Chess requires mental training for successful play. Attack and defense, tactics and strategy, talent, experience, and patience are all important components in chess. As you identify and thwart your opponent's plan, you must work to put your plan into action. While you may try to fool someone else, you're probably well aware that your rival is trying to do the same. The actual approach of a middle thrust is shown by the dodge on the wing, or vice versa. For these reasons, General Douglas Macarthur favored making chess an obligatory study for aspiring military officials.

Chess is an endurance, bravery, tenacity, and concentration challenge. This enhances one's capacity for interpersonal communication. It puts your athletic prowess to the test in a hostile setting.

Chess is a useful addition to academics and learning. Numerous studies have shown that playing chess helps youngsters improve their reading, math, and critical thinking skills. For these reasons, chess-playing kids do better in school and have a higher probability of success in life.

You can expand your horizons via chess. You don't have to be a top-ranked competitor to enter major tournaments. Even prestigious competitions like the US Open and the Australian Open welcome competitors of all skill levels. You have options to travel with chess, both domestically and internationally. Chess has a global language that allows players from all over the globe to converse on an equal footing.

As a result, you may meet intriguing individuals thanks to chess. Chess will introduce you to folks you could develop lifelong connections with.

Chess rewards those who are willing to dive deeply into its complexities with a continuous source of enjoyment and intellectual stimulation.

Chess fights are legendary since it isn't a typical sport. The game has excellent mechanics but troublesome traps and assaults. The idea behind the chess set is that the king is the most prized piece on the chessboard. If a player announces a check, protecting the king at all costs takes precedence. The game ends, and you lose a verification officer if you cannot rescue the king.

As much as playing chess is for fun, seriousness and concentration are also important; therefore, the more serious you are, the more focused you are.

Playing games is a fantastic way to improve your chess. The more chess you play and more experience you get, the more you learn and get to know the game. As your memory increases, the more you play, the more you'll learn to examine your plays and methods at a new level.

Chess machine strategies may help you improve the game while giving your opponent an advantage. Remember the functions, use all available opportunities, and your skills will significantly increase.

You now know the fundamental ideas behind chess, as well as how to play it. Chess is an extremely complicated game;

therefore, learning it requires much more than just reading about it. Playing, losing, and learning are the greatest methods to enhance your game. Take your time and put in as much training as you can. You will rapidly improve as a chess player with more practice. You are a skilled player who will become a winning player with practice. Bring out you're a chess set and challenge a player on your level. Good Luck!

Thank you from the bottom of my heart for choosing to read this book!

It is with immense gratitude that I address these words to you. It gives me enormous pleasure to know that you have decided to give your time and attention to these pages that I have written with commitment and dedication.

Creating this book has been an exciting journey, and my hope is that you have found it as enjoyable and inspiring to read as I have in writing it. Every word was carefully chosen with the goal of conveying a message, a story or a new perspective to you.

I am aware that you have a multitude of choices available to you when it comes to books, and the fact that you chose mine is a source of great pride and happiness. Your choice is invaluable to me, as it is the support and interest of readers like you that give meaning to my work as a writer.

If you have enjoyed the journey you have taken with these pages, I kindly ask you to **share your experience with others**. Reader reviews are a vital tool for raising awareness of a book and helping other readers make an informed choice.

If you feel inspired to do so, you might **take a few minutes to write a positive review** in which you could share your opinions. Even a few words can make a huge difference and help introduce the book to a wider audience.

Made in the USA
Monee, IL
24 October 2023

45138560R00070